the**selection**
interview

PENNY HACKETT

Penny Hackett has many years' experience of personnel and training as a practitioner, lecturer, and consultant. Now working for Clarks International, based in Somerset, she is the author of a number of books and articles, including *Introduction to Training* (1997), published by the Chartered Institute of Personnel and Development.

Management Shapers is a comprehensive series covering all the crucial management skill areas. Each book includes the key issues, helpful starting points and practical advice in a concise and lively style. Together, they form an accessible library reflecting current best practice – ideal for study or quick reference.

The Chartered Institute of Personnel and Development is the leading publisher of books and reports for personnel and training professionals, students, and all those concerned with the effective management and development of people at work. For full details of all our titles, please contact the Publishing Department:

tel. 020-8263 3387
fax 020-8263 3850
e-mail publish@cipd.co.uk

The catalogue of all CIPD titles can be viewed on the CIPD website:
www.cipd.co.uk/bookstore

the**selection** interview

PENNY HACKETT

Chartered Institute of Personnel and Development

First published in the *Training Extras* series in 1995
Reprinted 1997
First published in the *Management Shapers* series in 1998
Reprinted 1999, 2003

Design by Curve
Typesetting by Paperweight
Printed in Great Britain by
The Cromwell Press, Trowbridge, Wiltshire

British Library Cataloguing in Publication Data
A catalogue record for this book is available from the
British Library

ISBN
0-85292-756-8

The views expressed in this book are the author's own and
may not necessarily reflect those of the CIPD.

Chartered Institute of Personnel and Development, CIPD House,
Camp Road, London SW19 4UX
Tel.: 020 8971 9000   Fax: 020 8263 3333
E-mail: cipd@cipd.co.uk   Website: www.cipd.co.uk
Incorporated by Royal Charter. Registered charity no. 1079797

contents

Other titles in the series:

1 before you start

Introduction

Interviewing is not the *only* way to assess suitability for a particular job. On its own, it is not even the *best* way. In the hands of those who lack the skill needed to interview effectively, it can be worse than useless. Even so, it is still by far the most widely-used method – and one in which every manager should be competent.

To get the best out of it, you need to:

● use it as part of a selection *process*, designed to take you from a thorough analysis of the job to a rigorous evaluation of evidence

■ *plan* and organise so that you, and others whom you wish to involve, operate effectively on the day

▲ use your own personal, interpersonal and analytical *skills* to make sure you achieve your objectives.

Our focus in this chapter and the next is on the first two of these. The remaining four chapters are devoted to helping you increase your confidence and competence in actually conducting selection interviews.

What are you looking for?

If you don't know what you are looking for, you may not recognise it when you find it. This applies whether the job you need to fill is new or well-established, an internal promotion or an external appointment.

So before you start worrying about the interview itself, take a little time to make sure the process you follow is designed to produce the results you require.

You will need:

- a *job description* or list of key tasks – to help both you and the candidate see what is involved

- an *employee specification* – to describe the competences and other attributes that the job demands

- an overall *assessment plan* – to identify which of the items on the employee specification are to be assessed during the interview, and which will be examined by other means – as well as or instead of the interview.

The job description

If you work in a large organisation, especially one with a personnel or human resources department, job descriptions are likely to be familiar, if not universally popular, documents. If you already have one for the position to be filled, make sure it reflects the job as it *will* be for your new recruit.

If there is no job description, you will need detailed guidance on how to go about producing one. You will find this in *Choosing the Players* (IPD, 1994).

Whatever your starting point, make sure that before you go any further with your interview planning you have a description or checklist to hand, covering all the following points accurately and succinctly:

●   **Job title**. This should clearly convey the nature of the work to be done. If the candidate does not immediately understand that your 'document diagnostician' is in charge of sorting the mail, you will end up with a mismatch.

☐   **Purpose**. Why does the job exist? How would the world be different if it didn't? One or two sentences should be enough to help you and the candidate get a feel for the overall scope of the job.

▲   **Key tasks**. You don't need a blow-by-blow account of *everything* the job-holder will do. You do need enough detail to enable candidates to see roughly how they will be spending their time and to enable you to work out the specific skills and knowledge they will need. Wherever you can, include an indication of the frequency with which particular tasks occur, the proportion of time they take up, and the standards against which performance will be judged.

● **Conditions**. Hours and days of work, rate of pay, and particular circumstances – such as travelling, nights away from home, outdoor work, or especially noisy or hazardous work – should all be noted.

Keep the description simple but comprehensive. Don't be tempted to leave out tasks that are difficult or frustrating. If they are part of the job, misleading the candidate is not the answer. Redesigning the job to remove or improve them could be.

Remember: the more realistic the expectations a new recruit has, the more likely he or she is to stay and meet your expectations.

The employee specification

Once you have a clear picture of what the job entails, you can analyse what it takes to do it effectively. It isn't enough to rely on 'finding another Jackie' or 'avoiding another Michael' if they happen to be the best and worst previous holders of the job. You need to understand what it was that enabled Jackie to do the job well. And you need to know what Michael lacked.

In a big organisation, the personnel or recruitment specialist should be able to help you translate the job description into a usable employee specification. Alternatively, you may have been trained to use a particular framework or system. If you are starting from scratch, you can compile one by answering the following questions.

Do you need someone who:

- **○** is skilled in operating or managing particular machines, processes or procedures? Which ones?

- **■** has specific technical, legal, financial, or other knowledge? In what breadth and depth? To what level?

- **▲** has a particular level of manual dexterity, physical strength or fitness? Where and how will this be applied? How sure are you that someone who lacked it would not be able to do the job another way?

- **○** is good with figures? What sort of calculations, from what sort of information, with what sort of equipment?

- **○** is good with words? Reading or writing, letters, technical reports, advertising copy or other documents? Speaking or listening? Presentations or less formal encounters?

- **○** is good at making decisions? What sort, in what time scales, with what input, and with what consequences?

- **■** has creative ideas? About what, how often, how practical?

- **▲** is quick to learn? What sort of things – practical, technical, theoretical? How – by doing, reading, observing?

- **○** gets the best out of other people? Individually or in groups? Using what sort of approach – directive or consultative, telling or coaching?

- works well in a team? Adopting what sort of role – chair or ideas person, driver or finisher?

- always sees a job through? What sort of jobs, in what time-scales, using what resources, with what support, and against what odds?

- plans, organises, and prioritises? His or her own work, or other people's? How complex, and in what time-scales?

- works well within a system, as opposed to someone who finds that constraining?

- likes to know the rules and keep to them, as opposed to someone who prefers flexibility or ambiguity?

- is able and willing to work on his or her own, making his or her own decisions and getting on with the job?

- is able and willing to drive? What sort of vehicle, how far, how frequently, to what standard?

- is flexible as regards working hours?

- is able and willing to stay away from home? How often, for how long, with what level of contact?

- has a particular outlook or set of personal values – in so far as these relate to work and relationships with customers and colleagues?

By answering these questions honestly and objectively you can:

○ prevent your prejudices getting the better of you. You are not looking for a man or woman, black or white. You are looking for a *person* who matches your specification. This is important. The Sex Discrimination Act 1975 and the Race Relations Act 1976 make it illegal to discriminate on grounds of sex, marital status, race or ethnic origin. Unjustifiably specifying a requirement that is less likely to be met by members of a particular group can discriminate indirectly

☐ plan your selection process to provide opportunities to assess every item on your list

▲ ensure that your selection decision can be based on systematic evaluation against clear and appropriate criteria – not just 'gut-feeling' or 'instinct'.

The assessment plan

Your primary concern is to assess the candidate. A close second is the need to make sure that candidates can assess whether the job and the organisation are right for them. Your selection process should be designed and conducted with the twin aims of:

○ finding out how the candidate matches up against the specification

☐ conveying to the candidate what it would be like to work for you.

Some of the items on your specification will be relatively easy to assess, others much harder. A direct question on an application form will tell you whether someone is qualified to drive a heavy goods vehicle. Determining whether he or she is a good team member calls for a more subtle approach.

The possible ingredients of a selection process are:

- letters of application
- application forms designed by the recruiter or *curriculum vitae* designed by the candidates
- pre-screening by telephone
- pre-screening by questionnaire, biographical inventory, or written submission of some sort – perhaps a draft business plan or other relevant exercise
- first interview – to draw up a 'shortlist'
- pencil and paper tests – of intelligence, personality, and verbal, numerical or other skill
- practical tests – of manual dexterity or co-ordination
- work samples – such as an accompanied drive or a presentation
- work samples from previous employment – such as (non-confidential) designs or reports
- trainability tests, in which instruction on a particular task precedes the test

- simulations – group or individual tasks designed to assess specific behaviour

- second interview

- references

- medical examination or questionnaire

- assessment centre, combining several of the above.

How many of them you decide to use, and in what sequence, will depend on:

- **Company policy**. This may dictate, for example, that all applicants complete a standard application form, or that references will be taken up by the personnel department.

- **Specific requirements**. Some of the items on your employee specification may best be assessed by constructing a simulation – perhaps a group task in which you can observe a number of candidates working together. If presentation skills are called for, a sample presentation may be a good idea. This can be prepared in advance or on the spot, on a familiar or unfamiliar topic – whichever best reflects the demands of the job. In positions of great trust, you would be foolhardy to proceed without taking up references. Where the nature of the work demands it, a medical check should always be included.

- **Urgency**. If you are in a hurry to make a decision, you won't be able to afford a lengthy selection process. To speed things up, ask candidates to ring for a telephone interview rather than submitting a *curriculum vitae* (which takes time to prepare and may leave out things you want to know) or an application form (which will take even longer to issue and get back). Consider inviting them for tests and interviews simultaneously – even though you might prefer to interview only those with promising test results.

○ **Resources available**. If you can assign and train someone to conduct telephone interviews against a checklist of questions, this may be quicker and more effective than the 'application form to first interview' route.

○ **Cost**. The more candidates you include at those stages – like the interview – which make most use of expensive management and professional time, the more costly the process will be. Pencil and paper tests, which can be administered and scored by someone else (provided they are properly trained), can help.

○ **Candidate numbers**. The larger the field of candidates, the more ruthless you will have to be in using letters of application, application forms or *curriculum vitae* to reduce the pool.

□ **Equal opportunities**. When time or money is short, it may be tempting to invite for interview only those whose application forms indicate a significant amount of relevant experience *and* all the required educational and vocational qualifications. In so doing, there is always the chance that those educated outside the UK, those for whom English is not their first language, and those who have acquired the relevant skills through an unconventional career path may suffer.

▲ **Candidate expectations**. Applicants for hourly-paid, relatively low-skilled jobs may expect to phone or call in person and have a brief interview. Any process that requires repeated visits may have a high attrition rate. Those who are still interested at the end could be those who haven't managed to get a job anywhere else in the meantime. For managerial and professional positions, on the other hand, failure to 'do the job properly' by putting candidates through a professionally conducted programme of shortlist and second interviews could deter the most able. Reactions to tests and assessment centres also vary. School and college leavers expect them. Others are more circumspect. All must be made aware of the purpose of the tests, and their role in the total process.

There is no ideal selection process. The best way to arrive at a solution that meets your needs and those of your candidates is to work step by step from your employee specification. Focus on the real essentials and make sure that nothing likely to make the difference between success and failure in the job is left unassessed. The pro forma Assessment Plan in the table on page 12 and 13 should help.

Start to think now about the kind of evidence that will convince you that a candidate does, or does not, match up.

Assessment Plan

COMPETENCE	TO BE ASSESSED BY			
	Form	Phone	Test 1	Test 2
operating skills				
specific knowledge				
dexterity				
physical fitness				
numeracy				
word-skills				
decision-making				
creativity				
ability to learn				
work with others				
team-skills				
sees things through				
planning				
system-oriented				
rule-oriented				
work alone				
driving				
flexibility				
travel				
personal values				

Sample	TO BE ASSESSED BY			
	Interview 1	Interview 2	Refs	Medical

Remember: don't be so preoccupied with what *you* want out of the process that you forget the candidates' needs.

Once you are sure of what you are looking for, and the overall shape of the process through which you will find it, you can start to think in more detail about getting the interviews themselves set up.

2 setting up the interview

Introduction

Your first task is to decide how many interviews you need each candidate to attend, and for what purpose. There are no hard and fast rules. It depends on:

- ⦿ the job
- ◼ the number and calibre of the candidates
- ▲ how far they have to travel to the interview
- ⦿ how many of your colleagues need to be involved in the assessment, and their availability
- ⦿ time
- ⦿ what other assessment methods are used – as well as or instead of interviews
- ◼ company procedure
- ▲ personal preference.

With the possible exception of very senior posts, two well-conducted visits to the organisation should be ample. After an offer has been made, the selected candidate can of course come in again to discuss points of detail about the job, the offer or the organisation.

The first visit is inevitably the time for first impressions – on both sides. You must decide how much further you want to go. If the selection process includes two interviews, the first can be used:

● as a fairly crude filter: to screen out candidates who don't live up to the expectations created by their application form, and to reduce the pool to a manageable size. Candidates who pass this hurdle must then be interviewed and assessed in depth at the second stage.

■ as an in-depth assessment: to screen out all but a very short list of maybe two or three candidates, one of whom has emerged as a front runner. The second interview is then a chance to confirm the assessment already made, and to compare the chosen candidate against other good candidates.

▲ somewhere between the two: to focus on the key elements of the employee specification in sufficient depth to ensure that only those who really have something to offer are brought back. The second meeting then provides a chance to probe areas that have not been explored, and to double-check on those that have.

Whichever you choose, it is important that the objective should remain constant for all candidates. If you interview the first half-dozen on the first of these three models, and then switch to the last model, you will not be in a position to determine fairly who should and should not be included in the second round. You could miss some good candidates or waste time on inferior ones as a result.

How many interviewers?

The answer to this depends on:

- who else will have to work with the selected candidate
- your management style
- company policy.

Involving your team

If the job to be filled entails joining a close-knit team, other members will probably want a say in who is appointed. They may be happy to do this at one remove, helping you to formulate the employee specification and selection process, and acting as a sounding-board for your evaluation of the candidates. They may want to observe the practical elements of the selection process and compare notes afterwards. Or they may want to spend time, together or separately, actually interviewing the candidates at either the first or second stage.

Involving your boss and/or your colleagues

Your boss or any of the other managers with whom the new recruit will have contact may also want his or her say. In some organisations it is customary for senior appointments to be made only when there is consensus among the senior management team. In parts of the public sector, volunteers from the relevant committees or governing bodies may need to be included.

Involving experts

For appointments requiring technical specialisms other than your own, you may need to seek help from an expert in the relevant field. If there is a personnel department charged with acting as custodian of the organisation's recruitment standards and equal opportunities policy, it too will need to be represented.

Panels *versus* one-to-one

With so many interested parties potentially vying for a seat in the interview room, you must decide:

- who *must* be there – and accommodate the others in planning, observation, or other stages of the process

- whether to interview all together or to set up a sequence by which each interviewer sees candidates in turn on a one-to-one basis.

If there is only one other person involved it can be quite useful to work as a two-person team. This:

- allows the opportunity for a more rounded assessment of each candidate. One interviewer can listen, reflect and make notes while the other develops a line of questioning.

■ enables you to 'cross-examine' each other after the interview to make sure that your assessment is based on firm evidence rather than on prejudice. For this reason it is recommended by both the Commission for Racial Equality and the Equal Opportunities commission.

But while two heads are better than one, three is definitely a crowd, and four begins to look bureaucratic in the extreme. These and even larger panels can be effective, of course, but only if:

○ the panel is very well chaired

■ there is careful pre-planning to identify each interviewer's area of interest and intended line of questioning

▲ all interviewers are trained in interview skills

◉ everyone is prepared to listen to every reply, to avoid asking questions which have already been answered

○ everyone is working towards a shared objective – selecting the right candidate – rather than developing their own personal or political agenda

○ the assessment of candidates is carefully structured to avoid panel members' building on each other's ideas rather than on what the candidate actually said

■ candidates are not intimidated.

Panel interviews can save time for the candidate and reduce the amount of repetition involved for them. Unless very skilfully handled by a team with a shared interest in the answers to all the questions raised, a lot of interviewers' time may be wasted.

If each panel member has a separate area of interest which is explored for only a few minutes of each interview, it will be better to pair them up to do a series of shorter, more focused, two-person interviews. Each pair can be charged with reporting back their assessment against particular criteria from the specification.

Where to interview

In selecting your interview location there are three main factors to consider:

● *accessibility*, for candidates and interviewers. Weigh up the relative costs of bringing large numbers of candidates to you against those of taking a small number of interviewers to the candidates.

■ *privacy*, to ensure confidentiality and concentration. It is possible to conduct an interview in a store-room or even on the shop floor, but unless you can do so without interruptions and distractions it would be best to look for an alternative.

▲ *workplace preview*, to enable candidates to picture themselves at work. Sooner or later they will have to know whether they will be working in a plush office with thick pile carpet and rubber plants – or in a draughty shed. If the shed is accessible and reasonably private, use it. If not, make sure your short-listed candidates get to see it *before* you make the offer.

If you cannot provide all three of these, put privacy first.

The interview room

Wherever you choose to interview there are a few things you can do to help get the environment right:

- **Lighting**. Make sure the room is well but not harshly lit. You are planning a business discussion, not a romantic assignation or a grilling. Think about the direction of the lighting, too. Arrange the furniture to ensure that no one has to look directly at the sun or other light source. It is not only distracting and uncomfortable but can make people feel they are under interrogation, and they may clam up accordingly.

- **Seating**. Choose chairs that are easy to get in and out of without undue effort or noise. Arrange them where you can see each other clearly but not too closely. Putting them at right-angles to each other rather than directly opposite creates a less formal setting. If there are two or more interviewers, think carefully about whether you want to 'take sides' opposite the candidate or sit in more of a circle. False intimacy never helps, but then nor does distant formality. However you arrange the seating, always make sure it is obvious which is the candidate's chair. If it's not immediately evident, leave your papers on the seat, or be prepared to sit somewhere else without drawing attention to it.

▲ **Other furniture**. You may have worked for years clawing your way up the corporate ladder to earn your big mahogany desk. You can choose to put it fairly and squarely between you and the candidates to let them know who's boss. Or you can come out from behind it for a while to get alongside the candidates and help work out whether they and the job are right for each other. Choose whichever is a truer reflection of your management style. If you mean to leap back over the desk and start hurling orders the moment the new recruit is hired, there is little point in pretending you are big on empowerment or consensus.

● **General amenities**. As more organisations introduce no-smoking policies, the question of smoking in the interview is less likely to arise. If candidates are not to be allowed to smoke during working time, there is no need to allow it in the interview. If you do allow it during the interview, make sure there is an ashtray to protect your flooring and the candidate's suit.

It is of course up to you whether you decide to serve refreshments during the interview. If you do, you will need somewhere to put down cups and saucers.

General administration

Once you have worked out where, when, and with whom to conduct your interviews, you still have a few more administrative chores to do before you get down to planning the content of the interview itself. You must decide:

● where you will ask people to report on arrival

■ what the reception procedure is to be

▲ whether and how you will reimburse candidates for their travelling expenses (this is more usual where they have had to travel some distance and are not being funded from other sources)

● which other elements of your selection process you will include on this visit, and who will be responsible for managing each

● whether you will include a general briefing about the job and/or the organisation or a tour of the workplace – and if either is to be included, who will handle it

● how long you will need for each interview: this could range from 15 minutes to two hours, depending on how much you are trying to assess

■ how much time you will need between interviews to write up your notes, do your final planning for the next interview and attend to other essential matters (10 minutes is the minimum you should allow; more if there are other people involved)

▲ how many interviews you can manage in a day (most people find it increasingly difficult to differentiate between candidates after they have seen six or seven in a row).

You will find more detailed guidance on some of these issues in later chapters. They are introduced here to help you plan your interview timetable and physical arrangements. Only when you have these clear are you ready to start inviting candidates to attend for interview. Do this:

○ by telephone, letter, or word of mouth, whichever is most mutually convenient

◻ making clear when, where, and to whom they should report

▲ enclosing a map and details of bus routes, parking arrangements, etc if appropriate

◐ outlining how long the proceedings are likely to take, and what and who will be involved

○ specifying what work samples, certificates, or other documents you would like them to bring

○ explaining your policy on reimbursement of expenses

◻ letting them know whom to contact in the event of queries

▲ asking them to confirm – to you or to someone you nominate – that they will attend

- including any other information that you think will help them at this stage, or that will enable them to find you, on time, and without adding unduly to their pre-interview nerves.

Remember: even at this stage, candidates are forming an impression of you and your organisation. Don't risk deterring the best through sloppy administration or poor planning.

3 interview strategies

Introduction

In Chapter 4 we consider the specifics of what to say and what not to say in an interview. Before we do that, you should give a little thought to the *structure* of the interview and the overall *style* you plan to adopt. This is important for two reasons:

● **Candidate reactions**. If your questions seem to dart all over the place or the candidates cannot see what you are driving at, they will become confused, defensive or aggressive. A clear and logical structure, which you can explain at the start of the interview, will help both you and the candidate make best use of time.

◻ **Consistency between candidates**. Unless you adopt the same sort of approach to each of them, your assessment of the candidates may be affected more by what you did than by what they said. If you found one boring and unimaginative, and another stimulating and creative, was it because you forced the first to take you blow-by-blow through his or her early education and work experience and allowed the second to select edited highlights to demonstrate a point?

Interview structure

The precise format will be determined by the employee specification. The amount of time devoted to particular areas and the sequence in which they are explored cannot be prescribed. But there are three general structures which can serve as a framework.

Biographical

This is the traditional approach and one with which some interviewers are especially comfortable. Taking the application form as your starting point you work either backwards or forwards, checking and examining key events. The conversation could go something like the one below.

> **Interviewer:**   *I see you left school at 16?*
>
> **Interviewee:**   *Yes, that's right. I would like to have stayed on, but my father had been ill for some time and we needed the extra income.*
>
> **Interviewer:**   *So how did you feel about that?*
>
> **Interviewee:**   *A bit frustrated, but I knew I could always go to night school, which I did.*

This exchange has enabled the interviewer to begin to understand a little of the candidate's approach to life. As the conversation progresses, further evidence – to support or alter the initial inferences – can be picked up.

Despite its wide use, this approach has several serious drawbacks:

● It can be time-consuming, particularly for older people. Even if you start in the present and work back, it can take some time to trace back through all the key events and form a complete picture.

■ It is predictable. Candidates who are aware of the weak spots in their career history will have their excuses ready. These may in themselves be illuminating, but could distort the picture which emerges.

▲ It is unreliable. You cannot be sure that all the positive and negative evidence you want will be revealed. If the interviewer in the conversation described was hoping to use discussion of when the candidate left school as a means of assessing ability to learn, he or she has not yet got much evidence on this.

● It puts all the onus on the interviewer. *You* have to select the areas for examination, without prior knowledge of what is to be learned from them.

Critical incidents

Instead of working through every stage in the candidate's life history, you can attempt to focus on particularly formative experiences. The conversation could go something like the one overleaf.

> **Interviewer:** *Could you tell me about your reasons for leaving XYZ company?*
>
> **Interviewee:** *Well, I'd been trying for ages to make them realise the market was changing. They just wouldn't listen.*
>
> **Interviewer:** *Why do you think that was?*
>
> **Interviewee:** *Well, they were pretty stuck in their ways. They'd been producing more or less the same products for nearly 50 years, and my boss thought he knew all there was to know. I really couldn't get on with someone so entrenched in their ways.*

Like the biographical interview, this line of questioning has begun to open up some insights into the candidate's past behaviour. Like the biographical interview, it has its drawbacks:

- ● The 'critical incidents' on which you choose to focus may not really be the turning points in the candidate's career. Nor may they highlight behaviour typical of the candidate.

- ▣ The activities and behaviours uncovered by this approach will not necessarily relate directly to the competences and attributes listed on your employee specification.

▲ By focusing on what appear to you to be critical incidents, you may create a negative atmosphere not conducive to a full and balanced assessment of the candidate. In theory, such incidents have an equal chance of showing the interviewee in either a positive or a negative light. In practice they tend to err on the negative side by picking out incidents that appear to require explanation rather than events that have helped to frame a career.

Criteria-based

The third and by far the best option is to take your employee specification as a starting point, and to invite the *candidate* to think of incidents and examples that demonstrate the key competences and attributes. If, for example, you are looking for someone who shares your belief that 'customers come first', the conversation might go something like the one overleaf.

Through this line of questioning you will get directly to the evidence. To ensure that the picture which emerges is a balanced one, don't settle for just one example. Ask whether there were any instances when a customer proved impossible to satisfy, and explore those too. You should aim to get at least three examples for each of the criteria you are assessing.

At first sight, this may seem very direct. Candidates who are expecting to be guided gently down memory lane via a biographical approach will need a few words of explanation to help them see what is required. Most will then respond positively to what becomes a very purposeful and constructive interview. Provided the style you adopt is helpful not aggressive – see below – they will quickly get into the way of it.

Interviewer: *Can you tell me about a time when you really had to work hard to satisfy a customer?*

Interviewee: *Well, there was the lady who complained that my colleague had misquoted on her insurance policy...*

Interviewer: *What happened?*

Interviewee: *I had to spend quite a while finding out why she was so mad at us. I asked her to talk me through the original transaction step by step, and it became quite clear that we had misled her about the premium costs.*

Interviewer: *So what did you do?*

Interviewee: *I went straight to my supervisor and told her we must accept the customer's case and reduce the premium.*

By approaching all your criteria directly and explicitly, you can make sure all the attributes you need to assess are assessed. By allowing the interviewee to identify examples, deriving them from work, home, hobbies, education or any other sphere of life, you can be sure that every candidate has an equal opportunity to demonstrate his or her suitability.

Alternative styles

Stress interviews

Some normally sensible and capable managers undergo a personality change during selection interviews. Perhaps it is the chance to play God with someone else's career that makes them so aggressive. Or perhaps they have been interviewed that way themselves in the past and believe it is the thing to do. There is still a lingering school of thought that says if you need someone assertive and resilient, the best way to test these is to subject the candidates to a series of taunts, put-downs or challenges calculated to undermine their confidence or tax their temper.

Such an approach has three major drawbacks:

- It can leave *all* the candidates – even the one you want – with a very negative impression of you and your organisation.

- There is no evidence that ability to withstand this sort of attack correlates with success in any job outside the government intelligence services. The fact that people find personal abuse hard to tolerate does not mean they will be unable to stand up for their decisions, your organisation or its products when the need arises.

- Every now and then a candidate will lose his or her temper and assault you!

Tell and sell

If you are proud to work for your organisation, and if the vacancy is proving hard to fill or the candidate looks particularly impressive, you may fall into the trap of telling and selling. If you do, you will:

- talk for a disproportionate amount of time yourself – explaining the job, the organisation and all they offer

- find out relatively little about the candidates, because the focus will be on you and the job, not them and the employee specification

- risk making a wrong decision based on the candidate's reaction to you and your sales pitch, rather than on their ability to match your selection criteria

- risk talking someone into accepting the job, rather than helping to assess whether it is right for both of you.

If you really want to assess all your candidates fairly and objectively you must allow them to get more involved in the process. The best way of doing this is by:

- keeping your input to a minimum. Send external candidates written details of the job and the organisation before the interview. Alternatively, arrange for a general briefing for all candidates and perhaps a tour of the workplace. (This will be easier if the interview is part of a wider selection process and the candidates' programme can be extended to include it.)

☐   adopting a coaching approach to the interview.

Coaching

Think of the interview as a chance for some mutual learning. You each have a goal. Yours is to find the best candidate for the job and your organisation. The candidate's is to find a job and an organisation which is right for him or her.

The reality is that you have certain requirements and the candidate has certain attributes. By careful questioning – see Chapter 4 – you can raise your own and the candidate's awareness of the extent to which these match up. You can also help the candidate to take responsibility – either to accept the job and do all in his or her control to do it well – or to decide it is not right after all.

Once you both truly understand what the candidate can offer you and vice versa, you can explore the options. It may be that additional training would improve the match. There may be another role for which the candidate would be more suited. There may be other opportunities coming up in the future. If the interview produces greater clarity about what is right for the candidate as well as what is right for the job, it will have served its purpose.

More detail about coaching and its other applications are to be found in Sir John Whitmore's book *Coaching for Performance*, Nicholas Brealey Publishing Ltd, 1992. The benefits of such an approach are:

○ improved understanding of suitability, for both parties

□ greater commitment to the job by the chosen candidate

▲ more positive attitude to the organisation for the rejected candidates; this can be particularly vital if some or all the candidates are internal and are to continue working for you in their existing roles if not selected.

Remember: the interview is *not* a trial of strength or an ego trip. It is a chance for you to find someone with the knowledge and skills to help you and your team perform even better, and for the successful candidate to find a job that uses and develops his or her talents, gives a feeling of personal worth – and pays the bills. Focus on these goals and you won't go far wrong.

Creating the right atmosphere

DO

✔ Follow the guidance on setting up the interview room in Chapter 2.

✔ Allow enough time for each interview, so neither you nor the candidate will feel rushed or pressured. If you have only a handful of criteria to assess, as verification of other parts of the selection process, you may manage in 15 to 20 minutes. If you are attempting an in-depth assessment of eight or 10 criteria, you could need an hour or more.

✔ Make sure all your administrative arrangements work to plan, and that candidates are properly looked after on arrival – see Chapter 2.

✔ Put the candidate's application form, the job description, assessment checklist, some blank paper and a pen or pencil where you can use them during the interview.

✔ Make sure you know the candidate's name!

✔ Go in person to collect the candidate from the waiting area if you can. Address them by name to make sure you have the right one, and refer to the job for which they have applied. It has been known for candidates to end up in the wrong interview, which can be pretty embarrassing all round.

✔ On the way to the interview room, try to relax the candidate a little with a few opening pleasantries before the more formal part of the proceedings.

✔ Shake hands warmly and firmly. Resist the temptation to draw conclusions about candidates from the limpness of their grip or the dampness of their hands.

✔ Invite candidates to put their coats, briefcases, umbrellas etc. somewhere out of the way but visible, so they won't forget them when they leave.

✔ Make sure the candidate is comfortably seated and you can see each other clearly.

✅ Introduce yourself by name and job title. Explain your interest – eg 'I mange this branch of ABC company. If you joined us as a floor supervisor, you would report directly to me.'

✅ Thank candidates for coming. If you have not already done so, enquire about their journey and, if appropriate, explain when and by whom their expenses will be paid.

✅ Speak clearly but not too loudly. Vary both volume and pitch from time to time, to encourage the candidate to do the same. A normal adult-to-adult conversational tone is far better than a patronising parent-to-child one.

✅ Adopt a comfortable position. Vary it from time to time to encourage the candidate to do likewise.

✅ **EXPLAIN**   the purpose of this interview

its place in the overall selection process

its general structure

the approach you plan to take (the conversation opposite highlights some of the things you might say).

I'd like to start by outlining the purpose and structure of this interview, and say a little about how it fits into the selection process as a whole.

It's clearly important to both of us that we make the right decision – for the company and for you. As you know, this is one of two interviews you will be having, and there are also two written tests which we mentioned when we called to invite you for interview.

Each part of the process is designed with a specific focus, to help us get a full and fair picture of you and what you could bring with you to the job. In the process, we hope to give you enough insight into what it would be like working here to enable you to make up your mind whether this is the right thing for you at this stage.

So first, are there any pressing questions arising from the job description we sent you, or the briefing you had earlier today?… If not, we'll set aside a few minutes towards the end for some more general discussion on points that interest or concern you.

OK, then. In this interview I'd like to focus on three particular aspects: working with customers, decision-making and learning new things. We'll take each separately. I will ask you to think of examples of things you have done in the past which you believe highlight your abilities. You may want to choose examples from your school or college days, or from your hobbies or social activities, as well as from work. Feel free.

We'll start with learning new things. We as a company believe that we must continuously improve the way we work. That means we are all constantly having to learn new and better methods. Can you give me an example of something relatively complex which you feel you have mastered in the last year or so?...

What would you say you found most complex?...

Could you tell me more about how you tackled this?...

Was there anything in particular that helped?...

Were there any aspects that you never did quite get to grips with?...

What effect did that have?...

✅ Provide regular signposts to help the candidate see the relevance of your questions.

✅ Keep to a logical pattern and try to probe one topic fully before moving on to the next.

✅ Be alert for signs that the candidate is becoming worried or confused. You may need to slow down or explain yourself more clearly.

✅ Encourage the candidate to vary the choice of examples to cover social activities or hobbies as well as work or school. That way you will get a more rounded picture.

✔ Structure your questions simply and clearly. There is advice on this in Chapter 4.

✔ Allow candidates plenty of time to talk – encourage them with non-verbal cues like 'uh huh', or by nodding and looking interested.

✔ Listen attentively – Chapter 4 may help.

✔ Prevent the candidate from waffling or straying from the point by using words like 'specifically', 'particularly', 'exactly', to focus attention.

✔ Involve the candidate in the assessment process by regularly asking how he or she feels a particular example might or might not relate to the job in question.

✔ Summarise regularly to make sure you have understood what the candidate has been saying, to reassure him or her that you have been listening, to help you identify any gaps or inconsistencies in the picture which is emerging – and to help you decide what to ask next.

✔ Take notes – and explain to the candidate that you are doing so. Use your employee specification to record relevant examples and notes to aid recall after the interview.

✔ Keep your promise about allowing time for questions.

DON'T

✖ Talk too much. Resist the temptation to elaborate on your own role or history, or to re-run the job or organisation brief. If you talk for more than 30 per cent of the time you're definitely overdoing it.

✖ Get distracted. Even if the candidate did go to the same school, is a member of the same golf club, or supports the wrong football team, ignore it and stick to your plan. There's more on this in Chapter 5.

✖ Interrupt the candidate unless you really have to. Close down the more talkative by nodding quickly. Try producing a very succinct summary of a long and rambling explanation. Without putting the candidate down, you may help them realise they have given an unnecessary amount of detail.

✖ Intimidate the candidate. Jabbing your finger or the point of your pen in the direction of his face, sitting back with your feet on the desk and your hands behind your head, staring eyeball to eyeball without blinking or breaking eye-contact from time to time, are all likely to make the candidate feel at a disadvantage.

✖ Let your physical mannerisms distract the candidate. Fiddling with papers, jewellery, furniture or other items will draw their attention and make it harder to think of the examples you need.

- ✖ Sit absolutely still as though rigor mortis had set in. To help the candidate relax, try mirroring his or her posture, then gradually modify it to a more comfortable position.
- ✖ Attempt to complete complex checklists or score sheets while the interview is in progress. As long as you note key points and allow time afterwards for reviewing and organising your assessment, form-filling is an unnecessary distraction.
- ✖ Forget that each candidate deserves your undivided attention. That means *no* interruptions, in person or by telephone, can be tolerated – even under the guise of 'letting the candidates see what a madhouse this is'.
- ✖ Be too intense. You don't want your interviews to be a laugh a minute. You do want candidates to see you as a human being with whom they could work. Cracking jokes is not the answer. Smiling, often and sincerely, is.
- ✖ Overlook the candidates' need to know what will happen next. If they are going on to another part of the selection process, remind them who they will be meeting and what for. If they will be leaving at the end of the interview, make sure you explain what will happen next – and by when.

4 questioning techniques

Introduction

With a clear employee specification, a criteria-based strategy and a coaching approach, you will not find it difficult to work out what questions you need answered. You *will* need to think how to phrase your questions to maximise the chances of finding out exactly what you need to know, efficiently and pleasantly.

There are two main types of question and a number of variations. By using each appropriately you will be able to open up and close down the flow of information and direct it to the most fruitful lines of enquiry.

Types of question

Open questions

These invite more than a one-word answer. They usually start with:

'What …?'	eg 'What else were you aware of?'
'How …?'	eg 'How did you tackle that?'
'Why …?'	eg 'Why did you do that?'

The same effect can be achieved by phrases used as questions, such as:

> 'I'd like you to tell me about a time when ...'

> 'I wonder if you can think of an example of ...'

or by direct requests like:

> 'Would you enlarge on that a little for me please?'

If used as a follow-up to another question in this way, these questions are sometimes described as *probing*, see below.

Since the interview is supposed to help you find out about the candidate, it is sometimes assumed that every question asked should be an open one. If you can get the candidate talking and then probe for more detail, you should achieve your objectives.

In fact there may be times when you need to control the flow of information a little while you monitor its relevance.

Closed or direct questions

These invite only a one-word or very brief answer. They often start with:

'When...?'	eg 'When was that?'
'Where ...?'	eg 'Where were you based?'
'Who ...?'	eg 'Who else was involved?'

'How ...?'   eg 'How many times did that happen?'

The replies are likely to be explicit and factual – a date, a place, a name, a number.

Equally succinct responses will be elicited by direct YES/NO questions. These may start:

'Did you ...?'

'Have you ...?'

'Could you ...?'

'Will you...?'

The replies should tell you whether the candidate did or didn't, has or hasn't.

It is easy to become obsessive about the structure of questions and the distinction between open and closed. If you look carefully at some of the examples in the *Open* section above, you will see that their precise wording is in fact closed. When asked

'Would you enlarge on that a little for me, please?'

the candidate could of course say no. It is unlikely that they *will* if the tone of the question and the context suggest that something more is called for.

Judicious use of closed questions helps to clarify or confirm factual data. It also speeds up the pace of a slow-moving interview. They are therefore rather more useful than they might appear at first sight. Where they can be counterproductive is where the candidate is already inclined to staccato replies. Then you really will have to provide every encouragement for him or her to open up.

Leading questions

Variants of the closed question, leading questions are to be avoided at all costs. You may think you know what you want the candidate to say. Constructing your questions in a way that makes this a foregone conclusion adds nothing to the assessment. Questions which state or imply 'You do, don't you?' demand the answer yes. Those that are phrased 'You don't, do you?' demand a no. Avoid them unless you really do just want to see whether the candidate will contradict you.

Multiple questions

In trying to make your questions clear and easy to understand you may find yourself amplifying what started off as a simply worded question. When this happens, you will probably end up with a multiple question. For instance:

> 'I'd like you to give me an example of something you found particularly hard to master … I mean something you tried to learn that you found difficult to understand, or perhaps something that you feel you learned in theory but then found hard to apply.'

The candidate is faced with a choice of questions – and you may find it hard to interpret the reply.

Try to avoid such confusion. Ask one question at a time.

Probing
Whatever type of question you have asked, never be frightened to seek a more detailed understanding. Don't feel inhibited from asking:

'What else?'

'What then?'

'What do you put that down to?'

'What influenced you?'

or any other question that gets you closer to the situations described by the candidate. If a very positive picture is being painted, probe to see if there is another side to the story. If the picture that is emerging appears negative, be equally rigorous in probing for examples or information that may counterbalance this.

Questions to ask

Most of your questions will be dictated by your employee specification. Others should already have been answered by a well-designed application form. There are just a few which it may be advisable to ask everyone:

'How many times in the last year have you been late for work?'

'Have you missed work (or been unable to get out) for any medical reason other than those shown on your application form?'

'Overall, how many days' sickness absence have you had in the last year?'

Answers to these questions will give you an indication of whether the candidate's standards of time-keeping and attendance are likely to match yours. If you are worried by the replies, or have any other reason to think the candidate has a health problem, you can either:

○ ask if he or she is prepared to undergo a medical examination

or:

■ ask directly about whatever is worrying you.

For instance:

'Have you ever used, or do you now use, drugs of any kind?'

If the job involves driving, don't forget to establish the number of penalty points on the candidate's licence.

If you plan to take up references – see Chapter 6 – make sure you ask:

> 'May we approach your present employer for a reference?'

If you are in a hurry to recruit:

> 'How much notice would you need to give your present employer?'

or:

> 'When would you be available to start work if we offered you the job?'

You may also need to know:

> 'Have you any holidays booked?'

Most of these direct questions will only take a moment. They can save a lot of time and frustration later.

One other group of questions worth mentioning is the 'test' question. If you need to know whether someone can cope with mental arithmetic, try:

> *'In this job, we would need you to be able to work out discounts and so on pretty much off the top of your head. I'll give you just two or three examples to see how you get on. Let's say someone wants to know what he'll have to pay for a £450 item with a 10% discount and a £5 delivery charge. What would you say?'*

Or if you need someone with a knowledge of geography you could try:

> 'In this job you would need to be able to identify possible routes for transport. If we needed to get a consignment overland to Turkey, what countries would be involved?'

Make sure you ask more than one such question to check whether the results are consistent.

Remember: such questions are only valid if they reflect the job itself. If a calculator or atlas would normally be available, or more time or other resources could be used, you must replicate these conditions – probably outside the interview.

Questions to avoid

Don't ask questions that might lead you to discriminate on grounds of race, sex, marital status or disability. Delving into the detail of people's private lives is both risky and unnecessary. Focus on whether each candidate is available for and competent to do the job, at the times when the job is to be done.

DON'T

✖ Ask 'Who will look after your children when they are sick?'

✖ Ask 'Does your partner mind your travelling or being away from home overnight?'

- ✖ Ask 'How will your husband manage if you're working on a Saturday?'
- ✖ Ask 'Do you plan to start a family/have any more children?'
- ✖ Ask 'How do you feel about working for a woman?'
- ✖ Ask 'How do you feel about joining an all-black team?'
- ✖ Ask 'You're not squeamish about pin-ups are you?'
- ✖ Ask 'You don't mind the odd bit of mickey-taking do you? – You'd be the first black person we've employed.'

Not all these questions may seem discriminatory. If you ask them of every candidate, you could argue some are not. The potential problem lies in the inferences candidates may draw from the fact that you have asked them. If they feel uncomfortable or suspicious about your line of questioning, that could undermine their confidence and mean they are unable to give of their best in the interview. If they don't get the job, they could blame you for asking.

Questions like this are also dangerous because you may jump to the wrong conclusions when you hear the answers. It really doesn't matter to you *who* will look after the children. The important thing is to make clear the demands the job will make, and to ask for evidence that the candidate can and will satisfy them.

This will be easier if the applicant is already working somewhere else. If so, you can ask about attendance. If not, you can ask what difficulties there may be in meeting your requirements. As long as those requirements can be shown to be necessary for effective performance, and not trumped up to deter members of particular groups from applying, you can explore with each candidate whether he or she is capable of meeting them.

The same goes for the other questions. Let all the candidates know the set-up, preferably by letting them see for themselves. If they do anticipate any difficulties, ask what you could do to help.

Potentially discriminatory questions *must* be avoided. Some other questions are less harmful but of only marginal use. As a general rule:

DON'T

✖ Ask too many questions about hobbies. If the candidate chooses to use them to provide examples and demonstrate particular skills or knowledge, that's fine. A brief question by way of opening pleasantries along the lines of 'Did you see the big match on Saturday?' should do no harm. But for many people, hobbies are an antidote to their working lives. Writing the chess-player or rambler off as introvert, or rating the oarsman as a good team player may be wholly inappropriate. And membership of the right (or wrong) club is definitely not something you should take into account – see Chapter 5.

✖ Ask too many questions about health. If the candidate does have a medical problem, that does not automatically rule him or her out. Unless you are a doctor you can't hope to assess whether a specific form of epilepsy or a particular pattern of heart disease or mental illness will be a problem. Always seek professional advice.

✖ Ask hypothetical questions like 'What do you think you would do if…?' What candidates think they would do and what they actually would do could be quite different. Focusing on what a candidate did do when a situation calling for the same competences arose is a much better guide.

✖ Ask questions to assess attributes better assessed by other methods. If presentation skills are important, don't rely on the candidate's second-hand account of a recent presentation – ask for a sample now. If numeracy is vital, test it – either during the interview as outlined above, or in a separate pencil and paper exercise, whichever is more appropriate to the type of competence required.

Candidates' questions

Make sure you really do leave time to answer any legitimate questions the candidate wants to ask of you – and that you have the facts at your fingertips to do so accurately and authoritatively.

Remember: any information you give could later be taken to be part of the contract of employment. Make sure you, and your company, will stand by any promises made. Typical questions include:

- ● 'When do you need someone to start?'

- ■ 'What sort of training will you give?'

- ▲ 'What are the career prospects?'

- ● 'What would be the chances of working abroad?'

- ● 'Would you allow day-release to study?'

- ● 'It said in the local paper you were making people redundant. Will this job be affected?'

- ■ 'Do you have an equal opportunities policy?'

- ▲ 'Do you have an environmental policy?'

- ● 'Can I get an NVQ (National Vocational Qualification) working here?'

- ● 'What time would I start and finish work?'

- ● 'Are holidays taken at fixed times of year?'

- ■ 'Do you pay weekly or monthly – in cash, or by bank transfer?'

And you may have to produce a host of other specifics about any terms and conditions you have not already explained. Even if you have given a full briefing about the job and the organisation, expect the keener candidates to have at least a couple of questions each. Most interviewee training programmes advocate this as a means of showing interest and commitment.

The questions chosen can themselves be quite illuminating. Watch for those who are more interested in what they will get out of the job than in what they will put into it.

Remember: an effective interview is more than just a series of questions and answers. Unless both parties are listening carefully and weighing up what they are hearing, it will be a futile exercise.

5 listening and evaluating

Introduction

Often you will be aware that you are only half listening. The car radio does (or should) not claim your full attention when you are driving. Many people read the newspaper, cook, or do the ironing while apparently listening to radio, TV, family or friends.

The quality of listening on such occasions is unlikely to be at the level needed to make the most of a selection interview. For that you need real concentration and awareness. Many things conspire to make this difficult.

Barriers to listening

- **Noise**. Loud or distracting noises, particularly ringing telephones, whirring machinery, other conversations, or sudden aircraft or traffic noise make it hard to maintain an appropriate level of concentration and may even blot out what the candidate is saying. Even if you are used to them, the candidate may not be.

- **Movement**. Unexpected movements – people entering the room, vehicles crossing your line of vision – can distract for long enough to destroy your train of thought.

▲ **Mental distractions**. The pile of correspondence you can see on your desk, the half-written report you've been struggling with for days, the appointment you forgot first thing this morning, the appraisal interview your boss is planning for you tomorrow, the groceries you've got to buy on the way home, the telephone call you need to make before lunch – these and a thousand and one other items can occupy parts of your attention, leaving less for the candidate. If you have personal or business problems greater than these routine items, the distraction will be all the more damaging.

● **Physical distractions**. Tiredness, ill health, or even an uncomfortable sitting position will reduce your ability to concentrate.

● **Candidate distractions**. The candidate who resembles someone you know but can't put a name to; the candidate who doesn't look as you had imagined from his or her application form; the candidate who says his or her golf handicap is in single figures when yours is far from it; the candidate whose car you collided with in the car park; the candidate whose coloured blouse is making you feel bilious – these are just some of the ways in which the interviewee can inadvertently distract you. Add the verbal and physical mannerisms they may have brought with them – a constant repetition of 'you know what I mean' or 'absolutely', a heavy accent, or persistent fiddling or fidgeting – and it's a wonder any interviewer can focus on the task in hand.

There are other more subtle barriers, too:

- **Anticipation**. You don't need to listen. You know what the candidate is going to say. This is a particular pitfall with candidates who speak relatively slowly or hesitantly. You find yourself wanting to finish their sentences for them. Take very great care. They may have been going to say something quite different.

- **Stereotyping**. This is an especially insidious form of anticipation. You start to predict what the candidate is *bound* to say. After all, he or she's that type. We will explore this in more detail later.

- **Lack of interest**. You have already seen a candidate who seems to match your specification. You can relax and switch off. Or can you? Don't you owe it to later candidates either to tell them the job is already filled – or go through the interview with as much attention and interest as for the previous candidate. This one could turn out even better. Even if he or she is only on a par, the first candidate may disappoint you later or turn you down.

- **Premature decision-making**. If the candidate said or did something to put you off early in the interview, it can be difficult to put that behind you and focus on gathering a balanced picture.

- **Inexperience**. When you are not used to interviewing, the effort of asking the right questions, in the right way, in the right sequence, with the right tone of voice and the right level of non-verbal encourage-ments, seems like a job in itself. Listening to the replies as well may be just too much. Yet if you don't, all the rest of your efforts will come to nothing. With practice you will master it all. Until then, if you have to interview alone, worry less about your questions and more about the answers.

Aids to listening

The best aid to listening is genuine interest. If you really do want to know what the candidate has to offer, you will find it much easier to concentrate on what he or she is saying. Beyond this, here are a few specific tips:

● Prepare carefully. If you know what you are looking for, you are more likely to be alert to clues that will help you find it.

■ Make sure your surroundings won't become a distraction. Put away, physically and mentally, any other task that may divert your attention.

▲ Don't attempt too many interviews in a row. You will find all the candidates begin to merge.

● Try to distance yourself from the dialogue, without being distant with the candidate. Imagine yourself watching the interview from the outside, observing the interaction between interviewer and interviewee. It sounds odd, but it can help to focus attention on what is being said.

● Keep control of the interview by homing in on specifics. Whenever the candidate seems inclined to ramble, request a specific example or ask how the one just given relates to the competence you are discussing.

● Make notes – but don't become so immersed in them you lose track of what the candidate is saying.

■ Force yourself to link each of your questions to the candidate's last reply. For example: '*You mentioned there were several factors which influenced you. Could you outline some of the others?*' or '*That example was drawn from your time at college. Are there any others, from either college or work, that we could look at?*'

▲ Maintain natural eye contact. Nod and encourage.

● Learn your own mannerisms. Some people tend to say 'I see' when they not only don't see but haven't heard. Any phrase you use habitually could be masking the fact that your attention is beginning to waver.

● Summarise at regular intervals. This really is the most powerful way of forcing yourself to listen. If you know that every few minutes you will have to give a concise resumé of what the candidate has said and the inferences you have drawn, it concentrates the mind.

Weighing things up

Your employee specification is the key to effective evaluation. Make sure you have it in front of you throughout the interview, and use it as the basis for your deliberations afterwards.

If you have sought several examples of how the candidate meets your criteria, review each carefully. What does it tell you? Are you going to conclude that the woman who left her job after a row with her boss is a headstrong and difficult character – or an independent thinker with clear principles?

Your conclusion will depend on the other evidence you have. If there were other occasions when she flew off the handle with those with whom she didn't see eye to eye, the first inference may be justified. If the pattern is one of reasoned debate and principled behaviour, the second may be nearer the mark. Whether she is right for you depends on whether her principles are in tune with yours – and whether she matches the rest of your specification.

Once you have worked through each of the criteria you set out to assess, you will be ready to combine this data with that from other sources. Before you do, you should check carefully to make sure you have avoided the pitfalls of evaluation.

Common pitfalls

We can never really know what makes someone else act in the way they do, or predict what they will do in different circumstances. The systematic and objective approach outlined so far gives a better chance than most, but it too will fail unless you are aware of, and know how to respond to, some of the most common pitfalls.

- **Snap judgements**. First impressions do count, but they are often wrong. Resist the temptation to put too much weight on the first few minutes of the interview unless you really need someone who makes an instant impact. Examine the evidence against all the relevant criteria, not just the physical appearance or interpersonal skills you register as the candidate walks in.

- **Negative bias**. One piece of bad news can easily outweigh three pieces of good. For a balanced view, you must prevent this. If there appear to be some negatives, don't write the candidate off or shy away for fear of mutual embarrassment. Probe fully to make sure you don't jump to conclusions based on half the facts. If you investigate further you may find the candidate emerging in a much more positive light.

- **Halo effect**. The candidate who scores highly against one or two of your criteria is not necessarily perfect. Beware of assuming that the snappy dresser is intelligent or that the articulate speaker has good interpersonal skills. Examine each of your criteria separately.

- **Horns**. The opposite is also true. Just because a candidate can produce no evidence to meet a particular criterion, don't assume it's a lost cause. If may be that there are compensating strengths in other areas.

● **Bias**. This takes many forms. The old school tie, the shared hobby, social class, age, physical appearance, can all colour your judgement and predispose you in favour of a particular candidate – who may or may not have the attributes you seek.

● **Prejudice**. The same factors which can bias you in favour of one candidate can prejudice you against another. The most insidious forms of prejudice are those based on race and sex – which are also illegal. If you catch yourself thinking 'I can't really see a woman doing this job,' or 'I don't think I can risk it with a black (or white) person,' take care.

The fact that the last woman you employed proved to be very unreliable doesn't mean that every other woman will too. If you pre-judge applicants as a group rather than assessing each on his or her merits, you risk landing yourself with an expensive sex or race discrimination case. You may also miss out on some of the best candidates.

■ **Stereotypes**. 'People whose eyes are close together are dishonest', 'never trust a man in a bow tie'. Generalising about people on the basis of what they look like or one aspect of their behaviour is potentially dangerous.

Whether the stereotype is physical ('People with red hair have quick tempers'), racial ('West Indians under-perform'), or social ('She's a real pillar of the community, definitely sound' or 'He's one of the lads; it would be good to have him on board') – avoid them.

When you have:

● planned your interview as part of a properly thought-through selection process

■ focused on gathering evidence against your employee specification

▲ conducted the interview in accordance with the guidelines above

● avoided all these pitfalls and given every candidate an equal opportunity to show you how he or she matches up

you are ready to start thinking about your final decision.

6 after the interview

Introduction

The data gathered during the interview may not be sufficient. You may need further evidence, from tests and other sources, to add to your evaluation. Provided your criteria were clear to begin with, combining data from several sources should not be too difficult. You should:

- ● rate each candidate on each criterion: score them out of five – where five means they significantly exceed the requirements of the job, three means they meet them, and one means they fall well short

- ■ apply a similar rating system to the results of simulations, tests, or other parts of your selection process, criterion by criterion

- ▲ integrate the assessments to produce an overall score against each criterion; depending on the weight to be given to various parts of the selection process, use either the arithmetic mean of the scores or your own best judgement – agreed with others involved in the selection: the table on pages 70–71 provides a framework.

Assessment Record

CRITERION	RATING		
	Test 1	Test 2	Sample
operating skills			
specific knowledge			
dexterity			
physical fitness			
numeracy			
word-skills			
decision-making			
creativity			
ability to learn			
work with others			
team-skills			
sees things through			
planning			
system-oriented			
rule-oriented			
work alone			
driving			
flexibility			
travel			
personal values			

Candidate: **Position:**

		RATING	
Interview 1	Interview 2	Overall rating	

Assessor: **Date:**

Cross-checking

Before you make a final decision, you may want to make sure the picture the candidate has presented is accurate. References from a previous employer can help.

Unless you have a central personnel department to take up references on your behalf, telephone referees with some prepared questions. These should be addressed to the candidate's immediate boss, if possible, and should include:

- confirmation of dates of employment and the nature of the duties performed

- details of number of times absent or late

- observations on work standards and general conduct

- reasons for leaving and the likelihood that the candidate would be re-employed.

Bear in mind:

- some employers prefer not to implicate themselves by giving a bad reference

- some employers will be satisfied with standards of work and conduct a good deal lower than yours

- some employers will be glad to get rid of a problem employee and may decide to be 'economical with the truth'

● some employers will have lost their records, forgotten the employee, or muddled him or her up with someone else.

Remember: other people's opinions are no substitute for your own rigorous assessment.

Making a decision

One of the candidates may by now have emerged as the obvious choice. Even so, it will be worth weighing all the evidence carefully. Look at the ratings you have given each candidate (the table on pages 70–71). Challenge each one. If others have been involved in the selection, make sure you all understand and agree the assessment.

● Study the results. If one candidate scores well on, say, six out of seven criteria but very poorly on the seventh, you may be tempted to take a chance. If the seventh item is critical to success, you may do better to choose the one who scores slightly less well across the board – as long as he or she at least meets your standard on each criterion.

◧ Beware of being drawn to the top scorer. Getting someone who is over-qualified can be almost as bad as someone who is lacking in key areas. Unless you can expand the job to make use of his or her talents, he or she may quickly become frustrated.

▲ Beware of settling for the best of a bad lot. If no one quite meets your standards, think carefully how much help and training would be needed to compensate. Can you afford the time and effort involved? What are the chances of success? If the shortfall is in an area difficult to improve through training – like honesty – don't do it.

● Don't be frightened to retrace your steps. Is it worth revisiting candidates not called for interview or screened out along the way? In the last resort it may be better to go back and start again, with a new advertisement and a new pool of candidates, rather than 'making do'.

If you are really unsure, you can offer the job on a trial basis in the first instance. Don't use this as an excuse for indecision, though. The only real benefit is the pressure it will put on you to review progress regularly, especially during the first few months. Don't be surprised if your chosen candidate is reluctant to join you on this basis.

Whatever the outcome of your deliberations:

● Make sure you keep notes of the basis on which your decision was reached. Your assessment record and interview notes will help. Check that there is a record of all the key factors which enabled you to make up your mind.

☐ Keep the paperwork for *all* the candidates for at least six months. There is just a chance that one of the candidates or someone acting on one's behalf may want to challenge your decision on the grounds of race or sex discrimination. This will be a lot easier to refute if you have clear notes, made at the time of selection, recording your reasons for rejection.

Advising the candidates

If you have a personnel department, check what part they want to play now. The tasks to be done include:

- making a formal offer to the chosen candidate

- arranging a start date, an induction programme, and getting the new recruit onto the payroll

▲ preparing a *Statement of Employment Particulars*.

If you have no personnel department and have to do these things yourself, *Choosing the Players*, by the present author and published by CIPD, tells you how.

Someone must also:

- notify the unsuccessful candidates, trying to leave things on a positive footing so they won't think badly of your organisation

- give feedback to any who asks, to assist them in future interviews. This can be particularly helpful to internal candidates. Make your comments as specific and constructive as you can. Highlight ways in which the examples given or the skills demonstrated fell short of what was needed for this job.

Don't get drawn into detailed debate about the rights and wrongs of your decision. Make it clear that it was based firmly and fairly on the evidence presented during the selection process. If candidates feel they have talents you failed to discover, suggest they may benefit from guidance on interview techniques so they will do themselves more justice in future.

Follow-up

Your decision may have been made and the new recruit may be about to join you, but your job as a selection interviewer is not quite done. You still have to:

● **Monitor the outcome.** Your personnel department may require you to do this so they can check the proportion of each gender and ethnic group who made it through each stage of your selection process. Even if they don't, you should start your own record to help make sure your assessment of candidates is not biased in favour of a particular group.

■ **Review the process.** Your interview skills are almost certainly capable of continuous improvement. There are a number of things you can do to help.

1.   Think back through the process as a whole and the interviews in particular. Identify any questions which

candidates seemed to find hard to follow or which failed to produce useful information. Were they necessary? How else could you have worded them?

2. Invite any colleagues involved in the process to give you feedback. Make sure they know what you were looking for and seek their help in improving your approach to uncovering it.

3. Once the recruit has been with you a few weeks, invite him or her to give you feedback. You will need a review around this time anyway to see how the settling in is going, to give feedback on progress, and to identify any further training required.

   Ask recruits to let you know whether they found parts of the selection process uncomfortable or confusing. Find out how they felt during the interview and what, if any, changes they would like to see. Take the opportunity to identify aspects of the job or organisation that have fallen short of the expectations raised at interview.

4. When you have observed the new recruit at work for a while, look back at your notes and assessment record. How would you rate him or her on each criterion now? How accurate was your original assessment? If you were well wide of the mark in some areas, try to work out what else you could have done to improve your accuracy.

Remember: interviewing is a skill. Like all skills, it can be improved with practice. That doesn't mean that the more you do, the better you get. It does mean a continuing effort to observe, review, and understand what happens before, during, and after your interviews – and working to improve.

Good interviewing!

With over 105,000 members, the **Chartered Institute of Personnel and Development** is the largest organisation in Europe dealing with the management and development of people. The CIPD operates its own publishing unit, producing books and research reports for human resource practitioners, students, and general managers charged with people management responsibilities.

Currently there are over 150 titles covering the full range of personnel and development issues. The books have been commissioned from leading experts in the field and are packed with the latest information and guidance to best practice.

For free copies of the CIPD Books Catalogue, please contact the publishing department:

Tel.: 020 8263 3387
Fax: 020 8263 3850
E-mail: publish@cipd.co.uk
View the full range of CIPD titles and order online on the CIPD website:
www.cipd.co.uk/bookstore

Orders for books should be sent to:

CIPD Publishing, Units 5–6 Industrial Estate,
Brecon, Powys LD3 8LA
Phone: 0870 8003 366
Fax: 0870 8000 100

Other titles in the *Management Shapers* series

The Appraisal Discussion

Terry Gillen

Shows you how to make appraisal a productive and motivating experience for all levels of performer. It includes:

- ● assessing performance fairly and accurately
- ■ using feedback to improve performance
- ▲ handling reluctant appraisees and avoiding bias
- ● agreeing future objectives
- ● identifying development needs.

1998 96 pages   0 85292 751 7

Asking Questions

Ian MacKay
(Second Edition)

Will help you ask the 'right' questions, using the correct form to elicit a useful response. All managers need to hone their questioning skills, whether interviewing, appraising or simply exchanging ideas. This book offers guidance and helpful advice on:

- using various forms of open question – including probing, simple interrogative, opinion-seeking, hypothetical, extension and precision etc

- encouraging and drawing out speakers through supportive statements and interjections

- establishing specific facts through closed or 'direct' approaches

- avoiding counter-productive questions

- using questions in a training context.

1998 96 pages   0 85292 768 1

Assertiveness

Terry Gillen

Will help you feel naturally confident, enjoy the respect of others and easily establish productive working relationships, even with 'awkward' people. It covers:

- understanding why you behave as you do and, when that behaviour is counter-productive, knowing what to do about it

- understanding other people better

- keeping your emotions under control

- preventing others' bullying, flattering or manipulating you

- acquiring easy-to-learn techniques that you can use immediately

- developing your personal assertiveness strategy.

1998 96 pages   0 85292 769 X

Constructive Feedback

Roland and Frances Bee

Practical advice on when to give feedback, how best to give it, and how to receive and use feedback yourself. It includes:

- using feedback in coaching, training, and team motivation

- distinguishing between criticism and feedback

- 10 tools of giving constructive feedback

- dealing with challenging situations and people.

1998 96 pages   0 85292 752 5

The Disciplinary Interview

Alan Fowler

This book will ensure that you adopt the correct procedures, conduct productive interviews and manage the outcome with confidence. It includes:

- ⬤ understanding the legal implications

- ⬛ investigating the facts and presenting the management case

- ▲ probing the employee's case and diffusing conflict

- ⬤ distinguishing between conduct and competence

- ⬤ weighing up the alternatives to dismissal.

1998 96 pages   0 85292 753 3

Listening Skills

Ian MacKay
(Second Edition)

Improve your ability in this crucial management skill! Clear explanations will help you:

- ● recognise the inhibitors to listening

- ■ listen to what is really being said by analysing and evaluating the message

- ▲ interpret tone of voice and non-verbal signals.

1998 80 pages   0 85292 754 1

Leadership Skills

John Adair

Leadership Skills will give you confidence, guidance and inspiration as you journey from being an effective manager to becoming a leader of excellence. Acknowledged as a world authority on leadership, Adair offers stimulating insights on:

- recognising and developing your leadership qualities

- acquiring the personal authority to give positive direction and the flexibility to embrace change

- acting on the key interacting needs – to achieve your task, build your team and develop its members

- transforming such core leadership functions such as planning, communicating and motivating into practical skills that you can master.

1998 96 pages   0 85292 764 9

Making Meetings Work

Patrick Forsyth

Will maximise your time (both before and during meetings), clarify your aims, improve your own and others' performance and make the whole process rewarding and productive. The book is full of practical tips and advice on:

- drawing up objectives and setting realistic agendas

- deciding the who, where, and when to meet

- chairing effectively – encouraging discussion, creativity and sound decision-making

- sharpening your skills of observation, listening and questioning to get your points across

- dealing with problem participants

- handling the follow-up – turning decisions into action.

1998 96 pages   0 85292 765 7

Motivating People

Iain Maitland

Will help you maximise individual and team skills to achieve personal, departmental and, above all, organisational goals. It provides practical insights into:

- becoming a better leader and co-ordinating winning teams

- identifying, setting and communicating achievable targets

- empowering others through simple job improvement techniques

- encouraging self-development, defining training needs and providing helpful assessment

- ensuring that pay and workplace conditions make a positive contribution to satisfaction and commitment.

1998 96 pages   0 85292 766 5

Negotiating, Persuading and Influencing

Alan Fowler

Develop the skills you need to manage your staff effectively, bargain successfully with colleagues or deal tactfully with superiors. Sound advice on:

- ● probing and questioning techniques

- ■ timing your tactics and using adjournments

- ▲ conceding and compromising to find common ground

- ● resisting manipulative ploys

- ● securing and implementing agreement.

1998 96 pages   ISBN 085292 755 X

Working in Teams

Alison Hardingham

Looks at teamworking from the inside. It will give you valuable insights into how you can make a more positive and effective contribution – as team member or team leader – to ensure that your team works together and achieves together. Clear and practical guidelines are given on:

- understanding the nature and make-up of teams

- finding out if your team is on track

- overcoming the most common teamworking problems

- recognising your own strengths and weaknesses as a team member

- giving teams the tools, techniques and organisational support they need.

1998 96 pages   0 85292 767 3